Ryan, Devon, "Alysadue", & Cara!

Merry Christmas 1990

I wish I was there to share it with you!

Have fun reading this collection of kids' poems.

Love all 4 of you!

Aunt Diana

Apples, Snakes, and Bellyaches

Calvin Miller

ILLUSTRATED BY MARC HARRISON

WORD PUBLISHING
Dallas·London·Vancouver·Melbourne

APPLES, SNAKES AND BELLYACHES.

Copyright © 1990 by Calvin Miller. Illustrations copyright © 1990 by Marc Harrison.

Library of Congress Cataloging-in-Publication Data

Miller, Calvin.
    Apples, snakes, and bellyaches / Calvin Miller : illustrations by Marc Harrison.
       p.   cm.
    Summary: A collection of humorous poems about upside-down noses, hijacked terrapins, Isaac Newton, and television.
    ISBN 0-8499-0690-3
  1. Children's poetry, American. 2. Humorous poetry, American.
    [1. Humorous poetry. 2. American poetry.] I. Harrison, Marc.
ill.
II. Title.
PS3563.I376A85   1990
811'.54—dc20   89-70628
                                           CIP
                                           AC

01239RGR987654321

Printed in the United States of America

Apples, Snakes, and Bellyaches

APPLES, SNAKES AND BELLYACHES

"One apple, one snake equals one bellyache,"
Said God, on a Thursday at three!

"Sssssssssee here," said the snake. "There's no bellyache;
Ssssimply pay no attention! Be free!
Show God who is boss…it's all applesauce!
Take one little bite and you'll ssssee!"

"This apple looks sunny, firm and not gummy—
I think I'll just chomp down and see!
Mmm! This is quite yummy and good for the tummy!"
Said Eve, standing under the tree.

After biting a chunk, she turned to her hunk
And said, "Adam, here, take a bite, too."
But when Adam bit down, he fell to the ground:
"I think I've come down with the flu!"

"Ha, ha," laughed the snake, "Tremble and ssssshake,
For you doubted the old ressssssipe:
One apple, one snake equals one bellyache,
Like God told you Thurssssssday at three!"

TOOTHLESS

Sir Hairy Green Tooth would not brush,
And so his teeth were never white.
Four large, fat germs lived in his mouth,
Some sixteen more bunked there at night.

But now the dirty germs are gone —
The uncouth, filthy little bums.
For Hairy's teeth are in a glass
And he can only brush his gums.

PIG LATIN

Publius and Portia Swine
Were happy Roman pigs of yore.
He cooed, "My lovely, darling sow."
She sighed, "My handsome Roman boar."
They married in a forum tent
Amid the lovely hyacinth.
A hundred thousand boars and sows
And cock-a-doodle-don'ts were there.
Tho' doubtful snouts were all about,
They oinked their promises with care.

"Do you take Portia, Publius,
 to be your lawful married grunt?"
The piggy Parson oinked.

"I oo-day," grunted Publius.

"Do you dear Portia take him, too?"

"I oo-day oo-tay," Portia said.

"I now pronounce you boar and sow,
And you may kiss each other now."
"I ove-lay ou-yay, Ortia-pay,"
Said Publius, the piggy groom.

"Oh, ee-may oo-tay;
I'll be ou-tray," oinked Portia to her boar.
"You handsome ine-sway,
Now you're ine-may
Now and evermore!"

They honeymooned two weeks in glop
And ate a wondrous pail of slop.
Stopping ever by the way,
Passersby would hear them say,

"Oh, Publius, I oo-day."

"Dear Oink! I oo-day oo-tay."

DINOSAURS

Dinosaurs?
They're all extinct, I think.
I want to cry,
I don't know why
The bruisers died!
Perhaps because their six-ounce brains
Were way back in their bony tails.

They had no prehistoric fears
Of all their prehistoric peers
Because (I hate to say it here) —
Their prehistoric mental gears
Were in their prehistoric rears.

Could we, you think, become extinct
By thinking down the drain
And deciding our decisions
Sitting backwards on our brains?

SOLOMON SORE LIPS

King Solomon of Israel
Had seven hundred wondrous wives,
And when he kissed them all good night
He puckered seven hundred times.

Although he kissed them at the rate
Of two-o-three-point-five per hour,
It still took three-point-four long hours—
Before his last wife was in bed,
And Solomon was nearly dead,
Overwhelmed by halitosis,
Lip-fatigued by puckerosis!

When Solomon first married them
He really didn't have a clue
(Although it made an awful racket
When the great horde said, "I do!").
All seven hundred nagging wives
Meant just as many pairs of jaws
And several million gripes and groans
And quite a lot of mom-in-laws!

At first he kissed frenetically,
But soon just alphabetically.
He'd kiss his way from Abigail
To Zelpha of Judea,
Taking two ten-minute breaks
At Bilpah and at Leah.

He mostly hated Thursdays,
For that was "concu-night."
That night besides his horde of brides
He had to kiss the concubines.
While "concues" were less favored,
He owned two hundred fifty-one,
So kissing them required an hour
If he kissed them on the run.

As Solomon grew very old,
He left his alphabet technique
And tried a different way to go
That he believed was quite unique.
And started with the ugliest
(To get the worst out of the way).
Then he kissed the sick ones
(Who had been in bed all day).
And then he kissed the ones with colds
And those with nasal hair,
Smooching rapidly along
Until he gladly reached the fair.

But kissing all the wives goodnight
Gave Solomon his greatest strain:
He kissed and kissed and kissed and kissed
Until his whole mouth felt the pain!

Each evening when his job was done,
Somewhere near three o'clock a.m.,
He always went straight to his bed,
Because he had to wake at five
To kiss them all good morn again.

I've heard that when he finally died
And went up to his home on high,
His welcome wasn't quite divine;
It made a chill run down his spine
To see a thousand concubines,
Standing puckered in a line.
He cried, "I'm doomed, alas, poor me!
I wish I'd married sensibly!"

SMOKIN' JONES

Mr. Jones smokes big cigars
Until his house sits in the smoke
And all the little birdies cough,
And all his little children choke.
They kiss him through the smoke and say,
"We love you, daddy—cough, cough, cough.
We're sure glad you're our—cough, cough—dad.
We love to be around you—cough—
Though—cough—the air is—cough, cough—bad."

Sometimes I see a cloud of smoke
Parked over by the Dairy Dream.
I know it's just the Joneses
Going out to have ice cream.
If you should see a moving cloud
With seven little pairs of feet,
It's likely just the Joneses
Coming down the smoky street.

A SHOCKING AFFAIR

"Minivey Cheever,
Are you a believer in love?"
Asked the slinky sweet pussycat, Simmony See.

Minivey cat purred to his kitten,
"Oh, my goodness, no! I've never seen love —
Or hair on a frog, or mushrooms grow feathers,
Or shoes for a dog!
I must make it clear to you, Simmony See,
I only believe in those things I can see,
And I cannot see love, so love must not be!"

"Well, Minivey Cheever," said Simmony See.
"I'm sure you believe in *one* thing you can't see—
I'll bet you believe in electricity!"

"Oh, no! You're quite wrong, sweet Simmony See.
I've never believed in electricity.
I can't see it, Simmony! How can it be?"

"Minivey, come to a socket with me."
Minivey did, and sweet Simmony See
Unscrewed the light bulb.

"I wouldn't advise this," Simmony said.
"You'd be smarter my dear, if you'd use your head.
There's stuff in this socket to knock you clear dead."

"I'll never believe it," the tomcat assailed!
As Simmony jammed his beautiful tail
Into the socket! Wow! What a wail!

Then a curious thing began to occur.
Minivey's eyebrows stuck out like his fur.
And his eyes both lit up like two flashing lamps.
His hair "spronged" in frizzies;
His muscles all cramped.
Sparks waggled his tongue and curled his toes
And crinkled his fur into an afro.

"Wow, at last I can feel what I never could see!
I, Minivey Cheever, am now a believer —
At least I believe in electricity.
Still, I've never seen love, so how can love be?"

Then Simmony kissed him right on his kisser
And Minivey fizzed like a July Fourth fizzer.
And a wonderful thing began to occur.
Minivey's eyebrows stuck out like his fur.
His eyes lit up like two flashing lamps.
His hair "spronged" in frizzies;
His muscles all cramped.
Love waggled his tongue and curled his toes
And crinkled his fur into an Afro.

"Wow, Simmony See, I felt your keen kiss
Clear down to my gizzard!
What megavolt lips, you high-voltage kisser!
Your kiss and your light socket left me inspired,
I'm going to marry and have my house wired!"

They married that day in a church by the sea.
Minivey kissed his kitty-to-be
And then cried aloud, "My Simmony See,
I'm a foolish old tomcat, too blind to see
That love is just great. And I fully agree
It's one of the real things you simply can't see!"

SEE THERE!

"There's something in the bathroom, Dad!"
I begged, "Please, Dad! Get out of bed!"

"There's nothing there," my daddy said.
"Come here, Dearie, and I'll show you,
Then we'll put you back to bed."

He walked me to the bathroom door
And then turned on the little light…
Something was in that bathroom!
It growled and ate us both that night.
"Now, Dad, see there, I didn't lie."
Growl! Roar! Chomp, chomp!
"Oh gulp! Good-bye!"

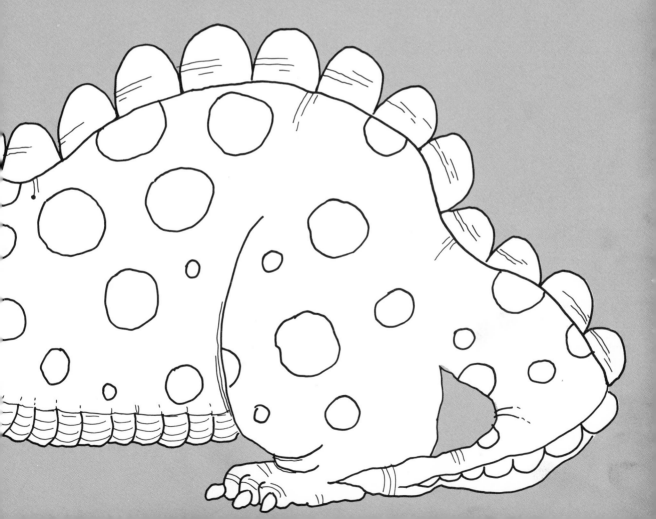

ANNIE AMOEBA

Annie Amoeba was rather attractive
For a shapeless blob who rolled all around
With her nucleus showing.
She appeared on the CBS five o'clock news
On Thursday, October the tenth,
And was asked very frankly,
"Just what do amoebas do all the day."
Annie was honest: "What else can I say?
We just roll around in a bucket of water,
Eating whatever gets in our way."

The host of the news show paused and went on,
"But Annie Amoeba, can you be happy?"

She broke into tears. "I wish I was dead.
I just roll about, living in doubt.
I just never know what I'm going to do;
I just never know when I might become two.
If my blobby body should grow long and wide,
I could any minute just up and divide
On the five o'clock news…
Oh my goodness," she said, "It's going to be…!
I'm going to be two…just watch and you'll see!"

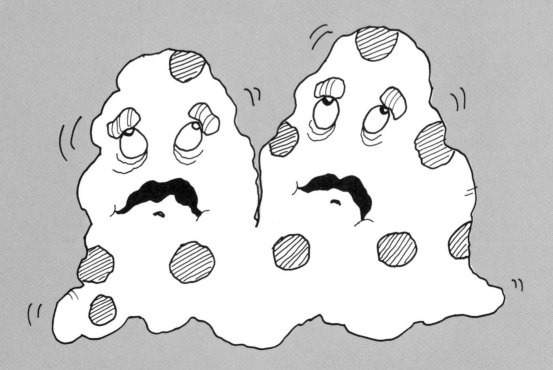

The host cried out, " Please, Annie-oh, wow!
No, Annie, not now! Oh, please, no dissension.
We must have your undivided attention."

But it was no use; soon Annie was two.
And then she was four and then, wow! Four more!
All eight rolled around the talk show, obscene
With their nuclei showing by five seventeen
Until coast to coast there were Annies SIXTEEN!
Little gray blobs who were soon thirty-two,
And then sixty-four — what else could they do?
They took over the network at five-forty-two.

THE PEEKABOO SURPRISE

One night old Sarah
Looked out at the trees
And swallowed the last of her
Fig cakes and cheese,
And broke into tears,
Wailing six "deary-meees!"
"I'm so very unhappy!
Abraham, please
Would you pray and ask God
If maybe…just maybe
He'd answer our prayers
And give us a baby?"

"Now, Honey," said Abraham,
"Don't make a fuss.
In April you're gonna be
Seventy plus.
You're getting so old
That you barely can hold
Your plate or your bowl
Or your saucer or cup.

It takes you an hour
Sometimes to stand up.
Forget about babies;
I'll buy you a pup.

Anyway, why
Do you want a new baby?"

"Maybe, just maybe,
I'd like to sing softly,
'Sweet rock-a-bye baby.
Momma loves snookums,
Kitch, kitch…kitchie koo!
Patty-cake, patty-cake,
Peek, peekaboo!'
And I want a sweet
Little baby to coo,
"Boo gurgledy boo,
Be bah nah gurgle
Goo gurgle goo goo!"

Then God sent an angel
With bright shiny hair
Who came down and cried,
"Hey Abe, are you there?
I must tell you true;
God's going to create
A great nation from you."

Abe scratched his head
And looked rather blue.
"You'd best hurry up;
My life's nearly through.
I'm old as the hills
And my Sarah is, too."

"Oh, yeah?" said the angel,
"Now, listen to me.
Your grandkids will be
Like the sand of the sea —
Far, far too many
To bounce on your knee!"

"Yeah," argued Abie,
"Just how can that be?
I'll sure have to bounce them
On bony old knees.
Besides, my sweet Sarah
Is all wrinkled up.
She sleeps every night
With her teeth in a cup.
I tell you the woman
Is babyproof now.
She's old—I say, old.
Her joints have grown cold.

And if she had a baby,
Then what would I do —
Play Little League ball
At a hundred and two?"

The angel just smiled.
He started to leave
And then turned to speak:
"Tell Sarah to check
With her doctor next week."

When the angel had gone,
Sarah saw her physician,
A Mesopotamian
Old obstetrician,
And said to him, "Doctor,
I've been feeling dizzy."

The doctor turned white
And then fainted away
And when he revived
He said, "My, what a day!
Sarah, believe me, you're not going to die,
But you'll have a baby
The eighth of July."

Old Sarah stood gasping
With nothing to say!
She, too, clapped her forehead
And fainted away.

And when she got up
She ended her stress
And bought a Chaldean
Maternity dress.

The months hurried by,
And at last came July,
And Sarah and Abie
Sang, "Rock-a-bye baby.
Momma loves snookums,
Kitch, kitch…kitchie koo!
Patty-cake, patty-cake
Peek, peekaboo!"

And sure enough, Isaac
Said "Gurgledy boo,
Be bah nah gurgle
Goo gurgle goo goo."

LULU

I know a horrid freckled girl
Who cried and begged to marry me,
But I said "NO" to her because
She's mean as mean could ever be!
She put her kitty's pretty tail
Into a blender full of rocks
And stoned her cat and buried it
Beneath the summer hollyhocks.

In every story that I write
I usually change the people's names,
But thinking of that poor old cat,
I'd better say it clear and plain!
They call her Lulu Frankenstein,
And while she is no friend of mine,
I freely give her name to you —
So if she ever calls, "Yoo-hoo!
It's Lulu, gitchy-gitchy goo.
Let's kiss; I'd like to marry you!"
Then run as fast as you would run
If she were Attila the Hun.

If you've an urge to take a wife —
A bride who's really quite a pearl —
You'd better marry someone else,
'Cause Lulu's really not your girl!
And even if she bats her eyes
And winks and smiles and sweetly sighs,
Don't speak! Just turn your back and walk.
Don't hang around or stop to talk!
You could wind up among the rocks
Beneath those summer hollyhocks.

THE WEEPING HYENA

A laughing hyena I met in the park
Told jokes at the rate of some forty per batch
And laughed and slapped everyone full on the back
And said, "Do you get it? Hey man! Do you catch?"
But early one Thursday, he could not have guessed,
The laughing hyena woke very depressed—
"I'm living with burnout and six tons of stress."
His doctor then glued little wires on his chest
And gave him some twelve psychological tests,
Declaring aloud, "My dear Mister Hyena,
It isn't the stress that makes you feel greena,
We've just found a toothpick: it's lodged in your spleena—
The worst case of 'toothpikititis' I've seena!"

CARRIBBITT!

Fredrico Frog was very romantic;
Proposing for marriage was easy as pie.
But Mortimer frog was stumble-tongue-tied,
Awkward, self-conscious, and terribly shy.

Both of them loved sweet Contessa Toad
And took her to dine in a most formal bog.
They waltzed in tuxedoes and bright cummerbunds
And spoke of romance on a glistening log.

They drank pure delight from buttercup cups
And gazed their love beams through each slitted eye.
Each ate from a plate — a sleek lily leaf —
Rich souffle of gnat and fillet of fly.

Fredrico at last croaked sweetly, "Contessa,
From the tip of your head to the webs of your dance,
You're toadly angelic, amphibian class—
The green-spotted hope of my froggish romance."

Mortimer shifted, painfully searching.
Contessa tried hard to pluck up his grit.

"Mortimer, darling, what do you say?"
He said, shyly blushing, "Carribbitt!"

Fredrico went on: "I'm a frog politician —
Suave hopper, whose hopping is marked with ambition.
I'll drive you to parliament in a Rolls-Royce
With nickel hubcaps and a silver ignition."

Contessa's throat bulged; her eyes bugged a little.
"Mortimer, please, if you love me, admit it!"
A cold clammy tear crossed Mortimer's face,
And all he could say was, "Carribbitt!"

Which of the frogs did Contessa wed?
Ah, here is the boggy, sweet, swampy report!
Years later, Contessa sang sweet lullabies
Rocking a precious blue tadpole named Mort.

Fredrico, the playboy, was chatty-absurd,
So glib and so smooth he could always ad-lib it,
But Contessa admired a frog of few words:
CARRIBBITT, CARRIBBITT, CARRIBBITT!

ISAAC NEWTON

Sir Isaac Newton sure was smart,
Beneath the apple tree.
When one fell off and hit his head,
He said, "Wow, gravity!"

For Newton was a genius
And not a common slouch.
A genius cries, "Gravity!"
Most others just say "ouch!"

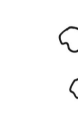

FANATIC

Mommy thinks that Mr. Jones,
The football fan across the street,
Is really a fanatic —
The very worst that you could meet.
He really loves the Lions and
Whenever they get badly beat
He fumes and kicks his TV set
Into the middle of the street.
Mommy says he throws it out
Nearly every football day.
He may be a fanatic, but
I really wouldn't want to say.

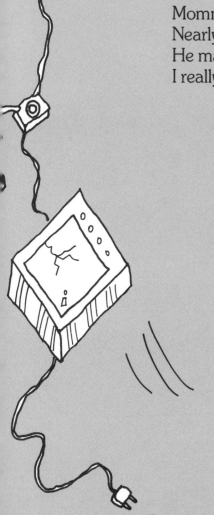

On Tuesday, mom was watching soaps
And boy! Did she get carried away!
(It was her very favorite soap:
I think it's called "The Edge of Day.")
She was crying in her tea
Until her face was ashen gray
And talking to the TV set
In a fanatic sort of way:
"Lorretta Mae, you're dumb, of course,
To force poor Horace to divorce —
You foolish, stupid, snobbish boob!"
She suddenly picked up a lamp
And smashed the giant picture tube.

I thought about my mommy then
As I went to my room to play.
Mom might be a fanatic, but
I really wouldn't want to say.

SIMBA

"Daniel…Oh, yeah!
Well I remember the night that they threw him
Into our den in the center of Persia.
I wanted to eat him right on the spot!
Nothing personal, mind you, it's just that our keepers
Had starved us for seventeen weeks and three days,
And I was so hungry that I could have eaten
A Mesopotamian, bracelets and everything.

Anyway, suddenly, there the man was — Daniel of Israel,
Lowered on ropes and dangling down to the stone floor before us.
When he finally landed, he simply knelt down
And started out praying like he was just saying a prayer
    before dinner —
A thanks for the food he was soon to receive!
Only he was the food here, and we were the eaters.
I'd never put much stock in God till right then,
But a much welcomed dinner that says its own grace
Can make even atheist lions believers.
When the food's kneeling there and blessing itself,
No lion with brains could doubt there's a God!"

Daniel was praying, but most unaware
That he was himself our answer to prayer,
To be sure…
He was less of an answer than we had desired —
He was scrawny and piddlin', gristled and meatless —
Bland as an unsalted, unpeppered dog —
Not much for a den of angle-boned lions.
Four was our number, and twice that our hunger!

First there was Leo, black-maned and thick-chested,
From South Abyssynia,
Caught as a cub and ripped from his mother
And mad at the world ever since.

Next came old Rex, a small older fellow,
Fur thinned for summer, mangy and elderly, bony from
    hunger, and wrinkled from age…
He drooled while he ate, yet never ate much,
Claiming a big meal was hard to digest.
Not much of a man-eating lion, I'd say…
(He'd not eat the whole man that got in his way).
"Old men," he said, "were just too nonsucculent,
Especially if they'd eaten spinach or mushrooms
Or any strong cheeses, like Limburger or Brie.

Rex insisted that cheeses were rat food
And often gave lions a mousy complexion.

Kimba was all a Numidian could be.
He loved to eat preachers just for the sport,
For preachers — he claimed —
Were the loudest of humans a lion might eat,
And thinning out preachers made room on the street
And helped God to keep his world somewhat quiet.

So there were the four of us, hungry and lean!

Why did the king throw Daniel our way?
Well, some said Darius was really a god.
The whole dumb idea was crazy to us…
Darius was barely five-foot-three tall…
Anyone looking could instantly tell
That he was no god —
In fact, he wasn't a very big human!
However, he did have an army and power
And could throw to the lions just about anyone
Who said that he wasn't all that he said he was.

We each one hung back in the shadows that night.
Skinny he was, but we "fourthed" him up fairly,

And while he was praying we walked up and growled…
He looked kind of sad-like right in our eyes
And said, "Boys, I'm sorry…I know you are hungry,
But maybe tomorrow night…just keep on waiting!"
And then he went back to his own peaceful praying
As we got aggressive and ready to eat!

We all roared a little and tried to get Daniel
To say an 'amen' so we could devour him
Without any conscience…'cause, truthfully,
We hated to pounce on anyone praying;
It made us feel so atheistic!
Still, he prayed for so long he left us no choice,
But to stop our wild roaring and shift into 'pounce.'
"Spring loaded ready" we were when it hit us…
LOCKJAW!
We were unable to open our mouths.

Daniel, it seemed, felt sorry for us…
I swear you could tell that he pitied our lockjaw…
He knew that a lion's mouth is his weapon,
For where there's no bite…there just is no lion!
It's simple as that!

Oh, we could have slapped him around, to be sure,
But since God had already locked up our jaws,
We feared He might just as well lock up our joints.
All things being equal, we decided right there
To growl through clenched teeth and just call it quits!

Well, morning came after the long night had passed,
And Darius came back to find Daniel praying
And not at all harmed.
Uneaten martyrs can make you feel great —
Like God's somehow bigger than you had supposed —
So Darius smiled broadly, looking very relieved!
It took quite a load off his shoulders to know
That there was a God who was bigger than he.

No longer responsible for the whole world,
Darius could smile…He was free to play
checkers the whole afternoon.

Darius and Daniel soon walked away,
But not till Darius had ordered his corporals
To throw down a few of the fat, extra wisemen.
And just as they lowered them into our pit,
Our lockjaw began to feel better at once.

Darius, himself, died not too much later,
Proving, of course, that Daniel was right:
Darius was really not much of a god!
But the real God that Daniel prayed to that night
Is still quite alive! We're the first to admit it.
For ever since the night of our lockjaw
We think quite a lot about God —
Especially at mealtime. And out of respect,
We never devour anyone who is praying
If anything else can be found for a meal.

TICKS

A tick'll stick his sticky snick
Into your gristle like a stick.
He'll hustle, bustle, in your muscle,
Sucking up a fat corpuscle.
Since ticks can make you very sick
Your first impulse will come quite quick
To pick the tick or kick the tick
Or flick the tick or stick the tick,
But never pick or kick or flick!
For if you pick a tick too quick
You could break off his sticky snick.
The snick will stay right in your skin
For seven weeks or maybe ten.
A tickless snick does no real harm.
But do you want to go out shopping
With a tick snick in your arm?

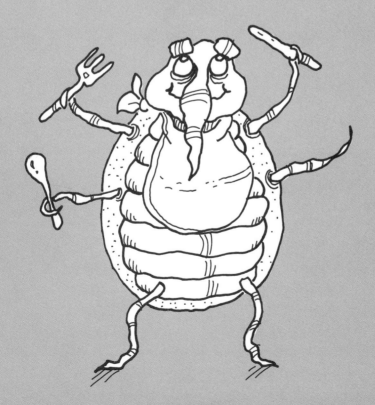

FUNNY FACE

Suppose my nose were upside down:
In any rainstorm I might drown.
The sun would shine into my eyes
Because my glasses sat so high.
One morning I'd hop out of bed
To find my mustache on my head.
And every time I'd sneeze or cough
The blast would blow my ballcap off.

THE EIGHTEEN-WHEELER

On the day that she was two,
Little, gentle Sarah Pooter
Was given a crash helmet
And a shiny, two-wheel scooter.
And whizzing down her driveway,
She pulverized her poodle.
"You stupid dog, what can I say?
You should have kept out of my way."

On the day that she was three,
Sarah got her first three-wheeler,
And ripping all around her town,
Sarah Pooter had no pity
And left some deep
Tricycle tracks
Upon a cuddly, fluffy kitty.
"You stupid cat, what can I say?
You should have kept out of my way."

At six, she got a six-wheel truck,
And careening through the Yukon there
She motored fast as she could drive
Across a giant polar bear,
Leaving muddy, ugly treads
On his beautiful white hair.
"You stupid bear, what can I say?
You should have kept out of my way."

For her eighteenth happy birthday,
Sarah got an eighteen-wheeler
And cried, "O destiny! O fate!
I, Sarah Pooter, will be great —
The terror of the interstate.
Now I can drive along and sing,
Leaving tracks on everything!"

But one day up in Washington,
Sarah met an eighty-ton,
Armor-plated sixteen-gun,
Fuel-injected, sixty-wheeler,
Napalm-breathing laser-spieler,
Driven fast as it would run
By an ape whom everyone
Called Attila, the Mongul-Hun.

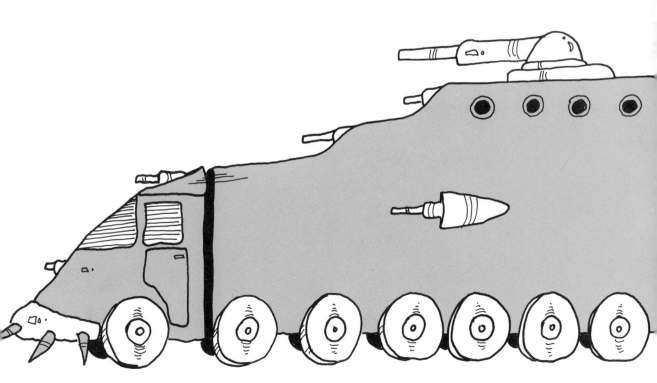

Attila and Sarah met
Head to head in such a crash,
The roar was heard in Calabash.
But Attila whizzed on ahead
And left poor Sarah almost dead
With eighteen stitches in her head.
The Semi-Hun called out and said,
"You stupid girl, what can I say?
You should have kept out of my way."

THIS SIDE UP

I'll bet you a big jar of raspberry jam
And also the strawberry milk in your cup
That no matter how long you practice each day
You can't drop your jelly-bread jelly-side up.
There's something in gravity, turns them around
So they always go splat with a splash on the floor.
As soon as you drop it, just wave, "bye-bye bread,"
And go to the cupboard to get you some more.
And if your mom screams that you've ruined her rug
With all of your upside-down jelly-bread glup,
Just bet her her knife and her fork and her cup
She can't drop *her* jelly-bread jelly-side up!

GUPPIES

Dad sometimes bosses mom around,
Then mom gets bossy with my sis,
Who bosses me so bossily,
I boss the dog,
Who bites our cat,
Who menaces our guppies,
Who always look neurotic.

And on the bottom of their tank
They gasp and bubble at their gills.
Their little eyes bulge, bloodshot, like
They've taken sixteen hyper pills.
If guppies had their way, they'd say,
"Look Dad, whenever you're despotic,
Please don't gripe at mom, OK?
For your psychological impaction
Always stirs a chain reaction
That leaves us guppies schizoid-tense —
Shaking in our bowl psychotic,
Goggle-eyed and most neurotic."

ALPHABET PROTEST

Have you heard that Congress might soon pass a law
That would change Ks to Bs and all Bs to Ks?
I'll tell you, I'm strictly opposed to such laws.
That would change everything that we must write or say.
Why, if all Bs were Ks and all Ks were Bs,
The parrots would sleep in Kanana trees,
And we'd go to the zoo to see Bangaroos,
ZeKras and yaBs with spots on their noses
And Boala Kears and wild Kuffaloes.

If this Kill is passed, our Krains will be corB,
The Statue of LiKerty will be in New YorB.
You'd better liBe eating your meals with a forB
And sandwiches made out of KarKeque porB.

Concerning vacations, I'll only say yucB!
Would you go to Disney to see Donald DucB
Or Minnie or MicBie Mouse? What rotten lucB!

This Kill would have mommies Biss KaKies goodnight
Or rocB them in rocBing chairs till it was light.
Koys would sleep in KunB Keds in their Kedroom
And Kig KlacB convertiKles sure would have headroom.
Do you see now why Congress must not pass this Kill?
ThinB of the poor souls who live in MilwauBee,
AlKuquerque or Bansas or those in BentucBee.
You must write to Congress on Capitol Hill
And say, "Leave our letters alone, if you will.
All Ks must be Ks and Bs must be Bs.

We voters demand that you listen up, please…
No federal tamp'ring with our ABCs!"

MISS RIB

One day when Adam felt very distressed
And so lonely he felt he could die,
God came along
And sat down beside him,
And Adam just started to cry.

"I've noticed," said Adam,
"That when you created,
You did it in pairs, by decree.
So how come as yet
I never have met
Anybody exactly like me?
I don't mean to gripe, God,
But begging your pardon,
There's no one like me
In all of this garden."

"Adam," said God,
"You need to remember —
I made you some duckies.
I'd say you're quite lucky!"

But Adam said, "Shucks,
I've had it with ducks.
Please make something new.
Something that talks
And says, "Hi, how-de-do!
Not like the mynas
And parakeets do,
But something that makes up
A sentence or two.
Something that could,
When I'm lonely like this,
Give me a hug or
A sweet little kiss.
Please, God, I beg you,
Make something like this?"

"Adam!" said God,
"It's a wonderful life!
If you'll give me a rib,
Then I'll make you a wife."

"A rib!" Adam cried
As he grabbed at his side,
"I don't mind your taking
A rib from my side;
It's your making a hole
That is ten inches wide
I must honestly say
I just can't abide."

Well, Adam lay down,
And when he woke up
At three ten or so,
He looked and saw Eve
And cried, "What do you know!

I'm Adam," said Adam
"It's not much to tell…"

"Glad to meet you, I'm Eve;
The name fits me well —
Not much of a name,
But it's easy to spell."

"Would you like to hold hands?"

"What good would that do?"

"Forget it, let's kiss?"

"Tell me this — what's a kiss?"

"Put your lips right on mine —
You'll soon get the knack —
Just pucker and slurp
And end with a smack."
They did — and the kiss
Knocked them both
On their backs.
"Wow! What if I take
You out on a date?"

"OK, I guess, Adam,
But what is a date?"

"It's where you go somewhere
Together, Eve dear,
And whisper sweet words
In each other's ear."

"Alright, it sounds great —
Let's go on a date."

So, on their first date
Adam picked her some roses,
And they stood for an hour
And laughed and rubbed noses.

Soon God came and said,
"Hello there, you two!"
They giggled and answered,
"God, how do you do?"

Then Adam said, "Eve
Is a wife I adore,
But I've still got twelve ribs—
Could you make me some more?"

"Whoa, Adam!" said God.
"That's just not my plan:
One husband, one wife,
One woman, one man.
Two women would be
One woman too much,
And one extra woman
Could get you in dutch."

"What's dutch?" Adam asked.
"Forget it," said God,
"Just go on a date.
Have a very good time,
But don't stay out late."

"Another date, Adam —
What will we do now?"

"Well, dear…let's see…
Um…what will it be?
Not much going on
Here in Eden tonight…
But I'm into romance,
So…I'll hum and you dance."

"That seems kinda dumb —
You dance and I'll hum."

"Forget it, we'll just walk
Around and hold hands."

"Hold hands again? Why?"

"Will you quit asking why?
So we won't walk around
With our hands flopping down."

And each night thereafter
They went on a date
And kissed and held hands
Though they didn't know why.
But the custom caught on,
And even today
You still see young girls
Holding hands with young guys.
And all those who do it
Seem not to know why.

HUMMING

I knew a little hummingbird
Who hummed Rachmaninoff.
But when his hummer grew too sore,
It turned into a cough.

He tied a mentholated rag
Around his long, sore beak,
His hummer had become too hoarse
To whistle, hum, or speak.

Without his hum, he felt so bum,
He purchased a kazoo
And flitted through the daisies
Playing "Rhapsody in Blue."

LEAKY

My doctor gave me sixteen shots,
Which left me full of holes and weak.
I asked him for a little drink
And found I'd sprung some sixteen leaks.

THE MICROSCOPIC SLEEZIES

Always wash your greasy hands, even when you
    see no grease,
For hiding by your fingernails, there's little things
    that you can't see.
They're itsy, bitsy, uglified and nasty germilated fleas
Called microscopic sleezies, who will sneeze
    and clap their knees

And hop and flop and flip and fly to any unwashed
    hand, and soon,
They'll linger on your finger, then they'll gallop up
    your spoon.
They'll leap ker-bung upon your tongue and
    snuggle in a cavity,
And springing from your adenoids,
They'll slide down your esophagee!

Beneath your slick esophagee
You've miles of rubbery pink pipes
    where sleezies love to sit
And, oozing germiletic grime,
    then stop a bit and hack and spit.

So if you wake up sneezing
    and your tongue is kinda green,
I wouldn't want to scare you,
    but these sleezies can be mean!

I've seen fifteen of them careen
Through kiddies' spleens in submarines
And plink their veins like rubber bands,
Make trampolines from rubber glands
Of kids who never wash their hands.

These sleezies sure love grimy knees
And scaly elbows, if you please,
And kids with short esophagees
  where they can cough and spit and sneeze
And give a kid who will not wash,
  their awful wheezy-sneeze disease.

BABY WALLABY POCKET

Poor Wanda the Wallaby grew quite afraid
When Wilma, her wallaby momma, declared,
"Look, Wanda! Get out of my pocket! Hop out!
The time now has come to be on your own."
But Wanda said, "Momma, I'm so very scared!"
And burrowed in deep and then hid out of sight
Till Wilma reached in and pulled Wanda outside.
"I hope all I've taught ya never will fail ya,
But Wanda, it's time to discover Australia!"

She pitched Wanda out, and she hit the ground,
Then Wilma and Wanda hopped all over town
And shopped for three hours till their pockets were full.
And Wanda said, "Momma, I've been such a grouch.
It sure is a blast being out of the pouch.
I have learned quite a bit from my wallaby trauma,
For no girl grows up when she's clinging to momma."

LAZY LONNIE

Lazy Lonnie
Set his alarm for six o'clock,
But when it rang and woke him up
He promptly slapped it off and then
Reset it to go off again
At seven — 'cause he felt so sour,
He thought he'd sleep one extra hour.

At seven, he was really tired
(Much tireder than he'd been at six).
He said, "Who cares — oh, fiddlestix!"
He set the clock right then for ten
And promptly fell asleep again.

This time he slept eleven days
And, waking really very late,
He barely woke up long enough
To set his clock to wake him up
On Monday, August twenty-eight.
And waking then, he set it
For November ten!

And then he slept till April three
And then again — oh goodness me,
I do forget — I only know
He passed away sometime last year.
His clock went off — he didn't hear —
And nearly everybody said,
"It looks like Lazy Lonnie's dead.
He died in sleep in his own bed —
A quiet way to go as such,
It's really not surprising
If you think about it much."

They tucked his clock into his box
And lowered him into a hole,
But just as Father Emmet said,
"God, take poor Lazy Lonnie's soul,"
The clock went off and Lonnie shook.
"I think I'm very rested now,
Anyway, what is today?
November ten! Oh, holy cow!
I'm off to school." he shouted, "Now!"
Out of the box he promptly leapt.
"Good grief, I think I've overslept!"

BAD WORDS

"Cheep, cheep, cheep...peep."
　Said Chuckie Chickie
　To his mother.
His mother shook and cried, "Cluck, cluck.
　I never want to hear, my dear,
　Another 'peep' come out of you.
　Chuckie, these four-letter words
　Will simply never, ever do.
　Do you understand me, Chuck?
　No more 'peep' words, I say!
　I don't care how urgent
　Or I'll wash out your beak
　With chicken detergent."

"Cheep, cheep, cheep...gleep!
　You'll never hear another —— — — out of me."

MACHO AND DELILAH

GOD: "Samson, I have given you
A body that is really tops.
I've only one instruction, son:
Please keep away from barbershops!"
SAMSON: "But even tho' I'm quite a hunk,
Won't the guys call me a missy?
Won't they flip their wrists and wink
And say that Samson is a sissy?"

GOD: "Don't worry 'bout that, Samson, son;
They will all keep still at best.
Your thirty-one-inch biceps
And your fifty-seven chest
Will quickly cause them all to see
That you are truly strong and right.
They'll meekly buy you bobby pins
And bring you curlers every night."
(Samson jogged to see his girl,
Forgetting all that God had pled.
I now repeat the real account
Of everything the couple said.)

DELILAH: "Where you been, Baby?
To the old health club, maybe?"
MACHO: "Yep!"
DELILAH: "Who does your hair, Hon?
Have you thought of a bun?"
MACHO: "I'm nervous whenever you speak of my hair.
If I like it long, Darling, why should you care?"
DELILAH: "Aw, Sugar, relax, I'll fix you some snax —
Some Gaza-Strip nachos — and Philistine fizzers,
With pinches of lime.
(I'll stir them with scissors!)"

MACHO: "Oh, I'd better get home!
Well, maybe one fizzer; what can it hurt?
I can grind men in the Philistine dirt!
Go ahead, Dee, and fix me a drink —
Something real stiff, like a Baal-Barracuda
What do I care, I'm Macho of Judah!"
(Samson glugged down the Baal-Barracuda!)
DELILAH: "Are you sleepy, Hon,
Just sit yourself there in that wonderful chair,
And put your sweet head with your
    wonderful hair
Right here in my lap — and take off that cap!"

MACHO: (Yawn) "I'm getting so sleepy,
I'm drifting, I think.
Did you put anything in that Philistine drink?
Did you drip me a slug,
I mean slip me a drug?
(Yawn) I'm slo seepy,
I mean I'm so sleepy,
I'm spurring my sleech,
I mean slurring my speech.
(Yawn) You sut down those pizzers
I mean put down those scissors,
ZZZZZZZZZZZZ."

DELILAH: "Nighty night, Hon! Here goes your bun!"

It just goes to show you when God wants his way
Even folks who have muscles and hair should obey.

ON HIJACKING TERRAPINS

A terrorist cat in a bandit's bandana
Hijacked a terrapin near a cabana
And ordered, "My friend, take me to Havana!
Do it right now — I don't mean manana!"

The dutiful terrapin started right then,
Moving as fast as a terrapin can.
But the trip to Havana took thirty-odd years
And nothing was left but whiskers and ears.
The skeleton cat held a rusty old gun
From the thirty-year trip that wasn't much fun.

If you have a hijacking urge, try a cheetah!
Its leopard-skin seats are really quite neetah!
Still, if you insist on a tortoise, have fun!
But don't try to hurry,
And do start out young!

SNAKES

Snakes have a bad reputation.
It's what they deserve, after all!
Some rattle their tails,
Some fan out their necks,
Some hang from the trees
Where you'd never suspect.
But all then crawl
And look sneaky and snakey.

Snakes prove that it's hard
To like anyone
Who lies in the grass
And sticks out his tongue.

THE ONE MINUTE
OLD TESTAMENT

In the beginning…
It was night
Till God said, "Pow!
"Let there be light!"
Then he made Adam
And his wife,
Who ate the fruit
And went kaput
And very promptly
Got the boot.

Once out of Eden,
They raised Cain —
That kid was rotten
In the main —
He murdered Abel,
Ran away,
And married…who?
We cannot say!
Some girl who lived
Out east of Eden
(Which is nowhere
Near to Sweden).
Then Adam said,
"Eve, Abel's dead;
We can't find Cain.
I think it's time
To try again."

They tried again
And in the main
Begot a very
Hardy strain
Till Noah came
And brought the rain
And sinful people
Were ashamed
To find themselves
Washed down the drain.

Then God called
Abraham of Ur
And said, "You'll be
A father, sir!"
Said Abe of Ur,
"God, I'm not sure.
Here comes my Sarah —
Look at her…
This thing could really
Cause a stir.
She's older than
Old Pharoah's setter —
And never been
A good begetter."

But they begat,
And Isaac came,
And he begat
(Somewhat the same)
A set of twins.
And Jacob who
Was one of them
Begat a dozen
Jewish men.
Jacob's Joseph —
Quite a man —
Left the ancient
Holy land
And down to Egypt
Brought the clan,
Where they camped out
Beside the Nile
And there endured
A life of trial.
In Egypt they begat
A mighty nation
With a little
Concentration.

When they'd been down
In Egypt for
Four hundred years
Or somewhat more,
Moses said,
"That's long enough.
Come now with me —
I'll split the sea."
And everybody
Said, "Gollee!"
From a mountain
Mose looked over,
Died, and Joshua
Took over.
And when Josh split
The Jordan River,
Caleb up and
Grabbed his liver,
Shouting out,
"Well, did you ever!"

For the next
Four hundred years,
The judges ruled
While thousands cheered.
And Jepthah called,
"Arise and fight,
You Israelites.
We'll show our might
To Canaanites
And Jebusites
And Perrizites.
We'll put to flight
The Hittites
And the Gittites
And the Moabites
And Ammonites
(But not termites
Or parasites).
So Gideon
Led the Gideonites
To war against
The Midianites.
And Samson led
The Samsonites
(Whose luggage was
So very nice).

Then came Samuel,
Saul, and David,
Who killed a
Giant Philistine
And later on
Became the king.
Then Solomon
And other kings,
Each one begat
Another king.

The Major Prophets
Came along
To tell the kings
When they were wrong.
And their rebukes
Were very strong.

Isaiah spoke
Of days to come
When all earth's people
would be one…

And then the king
Of Babylon
Waged war till
Israel was gone.

But they returned,
And Ezra came —
And rebuilt
Israel again.
Some Minor Prophets
Wrote a bit
Before God said,
"Well, this is it.
My Testament
At last is done,
And I must say —
It's sure been fun.
Then Malachi
Just happened by
And wrote another,
Final book.
God took a look
And said, 'Oh my,
You've done it well —
Thanks, Malachi!'
Let's call it quits!
The end! Good-bye!"

THE ONE MINUTE NEW TESTAMENT

Joseph the carpenter
Early one morn
Got married to Mary
And Jesus was born —
Though God and not Joseph
Was really his father.
Joseph loved Jesus
And so did his mother.

Then Jesus grew up
And was baptized by John,
Who wore camel's hair
And ate bugs and honey.
Yuck! He didn't care
If his breath was so bad
It polluted the air,
'Cause John sure loved God
As anyone must
If he says his grace proper
Before he sits down
To a plate of grasshoppers.

Then Jesus went down
To the shore of the sea
And saw Jim and Johnny
Bar Zebedee.
He said, "Follow me,"
And they did — as did others
Like Peter and Andrew,
Who also were brothers.
Eight more soon followed —
One dozen in all —
Round, squat and fat ones,
Thin, skinny, and tall.
Simon was dense,
And Thomas intense,
And Judas Iscariot
Straddled the fence.

For three years Christ traveled
Around with his friends
Till Herod and Pilate
Said, "This is the end!"
They hung our dear Lord
On a cross in the sky —
He gave up his life —
It made Mary cry.

They thought he was dead,
But their faces grew red
When he got out of bed
And walked from the tomb
As the lightening went "pow"
And the thunder "kaboom."
But soon he ascended
(That means to arise
And float up and away
Beyond the blue skies.)

But down came the Spirit
That first Pentecost!
His friends started preaching
To act out his Way.
This news spread like wildfire:
"He's home with his father,
But there he won't stay.
He'll come back some day —
He's gone until then,
But he's coming again!"

This news was so joyous —
So splendid, so grand —
Christianity spread
All over the land.
Saul tried to stop
The spread of the church,
But, alas, he only got
Left in the lurch.
"I'm going to kill Christians,
Put all of them down
And keep this religion
From gaining much ground!"
He stood up and blurted,
And he killed one or two
But then was converted.
And became an apostle
Just like the others.
But the others all said,
"Well, goodness me, brother!
You, Paul, are a mugger,
A real wooly bugger.
You can't preach here, Paul,
In our parks or our malls,
For as you see, Paul,
Jerusalem's home."
"OK," shouted Paul.
"I'll go preach in Rome!"

He did and wrote letters
To all Thessalonians
But not the Ionians.
He wrote the Galatians,
"Steer clear of temptations."
He made a decision
To write the Ephesians
And Titus and Tim
Who both pastored missions.
He wrote the Corinthians
And told them, "Don't fight,
You're sinning too much!
Behave and act right!"

Nero told Paul,
"Your life now is minus."
And Paul said, "You've got to be
Kidding, your highness."
But kidding he wasn't,
And so Paul was killed,
But went on to heaven
Immensely fulfilled.
And finally, then,
John wrote Revelation
And scared all his friends
With tales of damnation.
(For two thousand years
It's been a sensation.)
And that's all the Bible
There is now, my friends.
Amen, Hallelulah!
It's over…the end!

CORPUSCLES

There are some things too little to see, if you please,
That wriggle and wiggle inside arteries.
They vibrate and spin and go buzz in your blood.
They swim and dogpaddle and scriggle and shiver —
And do the sidestroke from your spleen to your liver.
And all through your body they hurry and scurry.
They all have red hair — but be thankful they're there
For by millions and jillions they make your blood red.
Believe me if they ever took the day off
In seventeen seconds you'd be very dead.

So the next time you say your nighty-night prayers,
Say, "God, I'm most grateful for these tiny spuds —
These little red doo-dads that swim in my blood.
And God, if you keep those guys swimming all night,
I'll get up and thank you as soon as it's light."

A NONCONFORMIST SPLAT!

I love to read the very book
That other kids ignore.
I therefore read the phone book
From Abbott to Zymore.

I never watch the TV shows
That all my friends must see,
I watch the weather channel
Till eleven thirty-three!

And when I hear of big events
Where the massive crowds have gone,
I always hurry somewhere else
So I can be alone.

Because my friends refused to jump
Off of a cliff today,
I, the nonconformist, jumped
I'm very proud to sa…a…a…a…a…a…ay.

Conformity, what's that?
Good grief…help…splat!

LOT 'N' LOTTIE

"I've left my best hat,
And I've got to go back,"
Said Lottie to Lot
As they fled out of Sodom.

"No! You'd better not,"
Warned her Mister Lot.
"For God said, my dear,
If you glance to the rear
You will wind up
A pillar of salt."

"OK," Lottie said
As she looked
Straight ahead.

"You can like it or not,
But I'm going back, Lot.
I've looked in my pocket
And can't find my locket.
I'm sure it's at home
By the bed."

"What good is a locket
If you've got no neck?
You better keep looking ahead
I suspect."

"OK," Lottie said
As she looked
Straight ahead.

"Further, dear Lot,
I can't find my ring.
I think it's at home
On the stand."

"Lottie, my dear,
What good is a ring
If you're only a salt block
And haven't a hand?"
"OK," Lottie said
And looked
Straight ahead.

"Oh, Lot, dearest Lot,
Know what I forgot?
Our Clearing House
Sweepstakes lottery stubs."

She then turned to go.
"No, please, Lottie, no!"

And Lot left her there
In the high desert air,
A pillar of salt
Not far from the sea.

Some say she melted —
By rain washed away.
Some say she simply
Diminished one May
As people filled salt shakers
Day after day.

All I know is that Lot
Just sat there and thought
Of his Lottie out melting
Away in the rain.
He decided salt-free
Was the way food should be,
And devoured his potatoes just plain.

HEADSTONES

Harriett Hausfrau wed her TV,
An adorable, twenty-five-inch RCA,
Her only true lover, since she had been three,
Watching cartoons through most of the day!

She sat and held on to the channel selector,
And gazed at her lover, quite smitten, I fear!
She watched, and she watched, like a G.E. inspector—
Ate thirty-eight truckloads of popcorn each year.

She died in her old yellow bathrobe one May,
When her picture tube blew and her heart gave way.
They buried them both side by side, so they say,
One headstone said Harriett; one said RCA!

FROST BIT

I just bought a triple dip
(Excuse me while I take a lick!)
Of Butter Brickle, Chocolate Chipple,
And Fudgilated Caramel Ripple!
(Excuse me while I take a lickle!)
It's impolite to slurp and lick,
But brickled-chips in triple-dips
Grow sticky-slick and start to drip,
Excuse me…lick…lick…lickky…lick…
I can't talk any more…I'll flip
Some chocolate slobberings…lick…lick.
Good-bye, lick, lick, I've got to run,
Lick…lick…I think I'm having fun…
My tongue is frozen and my lip…
Bye-bye! Drip, drip, lick, drip, lick, drip…

SKY-BARRED

Sergei, wing-broken, was one of the graylings.
He walked, feather-draggled, and dreamed of the sky.
He remembered the day his pain had been born —
The day he had waited high in the nest.
He'd waited and waited the flight of his mother
But she never came…never…she'd left in the morning
To fish in the shallows where fishing was risky.
She'd vowed to return to the nest before noon,
"I'll watch for the fox. I'll bring you your lunch."
But she never came.

The stars watched the night
Till the dawn light rose cold
And bleak as his hopes and stark as his fears.
He knew then his mother would never return.
And he knew he himself must soon leave the nest
Or starve never knowing the joy of the sky.
But his feathers still needed a week to be ready
And he poised full of fear on the edge of the nest.
He leapt into winds that tore his young feathers
And threw him in thrashing against the sea cliffs
Till he fell and he fell…it seemed into hell…
Before his bruised body crashed into earth
That forbad him to move.

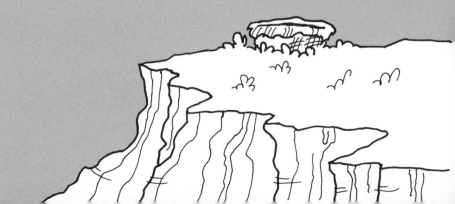

Sergei had cried when he first broke his wing,
But his tears gave way as he stumbled on rocks.
He knew anger by day when he gazed at the sky;
He knew fear by night when he hid from the fox.
His wing at last healed
But it never stirred air,
For his heart was more crippled than ever his wing.
His misery dwindled and shrank into spite —
Rehearsing his hatred
While fearing the night.
And thus in his anger he cried out to Zor,
"Are you God of the sky or God of mere sand?
Can you find any joy in the pain I endure,
Dragging a wing behind me in sand?"

Far from poor Sergei's broken-winged anger
In the High Crags of Skie on the Island of Life,
Sat Zor…wise old Zor, as the graylings all called him —
Gathering daylight to soften the night.
Zor's great heavy feathers seemed chiseled of steel,
His beak glistened lightning congealed out in space,
His talons were strong as cables of iron,
His eyes were ablaze with the fire of sheer grace.
He screamed to the winds, who hurried his voice
And bore it as whispers across the vast waters.

"Rise, Sergei, my son, and come home to me
Fear never the void, though the ocean be wide.
Though the crossing require all the strength that you own —
I'll order the sky to give you its wind,
Demand that the stars must call you their friend;
I'll speak to the sea to roar without foam,
Command the bold sun to light your way home.

But first you must trust—
Throw feathers to sky.
You'll see, I will meet you,
I'll be all around you;
I won't let you die.
Your dead wings will live—
You're going to fly!"

The wind whispered hope
All around Sergei's fears.
"Listen I may, but fly I may not.
I'm Sergei, the sandhobbler; hope I can't dare!
My wings rake the earth begging for air.
Don't mock me by asking what never can be.
Life for me is these warm sunlit sands
Where food lies low and abundant and free."

"Sergei, your food is the refuse of man!
It isn't your wings that won't work; it's your heart.
All those must hobble who will not learn trust.
Your doubt is a chain that binds you to dust.
Leap from the sea cliffs and call unto Zor —
Trust and your dead wings will stretch out once more."

"Sergei, my son, come home to the sky.
Trust and you'll live. Doubt and you'll die!"

For seven long days Sergei gazed seaward.
High on the cliff he would stare into gales
And pray for the courage to live above dust:
"I want to…I hate to…I need to…I must.
Will I die? Will I live? What's left for me here?"
He thought of the years and the fears and the tears.
He thought of his loneliness, anger, and hate.
He studied the rocks at the base of the cliffs.
He cried and then trembled, then leapt into space.

Seven days later, Zor heard a scream
And saw silhouetted against the bright blue
A wondrously marvelous, riveting sight.
"Sergei!" cried Zor, "Can this be you?"
"Yes," screamed the grayling, "I've buried disgrace."
Your throne is my thunder, your lightning, my mace.
At your word, I surfed the fringes of space.
I trusted you, Zor, and conquered the winds.
I've flown among stars and called them my friends.
You called me to flight and gave my eyes light.
You ordered the sea to roar without foam,
Commanded the sun to light my way home.
And once I had laid all my bitterness by
I leapt and believed — for to trust is to fly!"

GREASY

The fat man who married the skinny trapezee,
Loved watching her fly with the greatest of easee.
But she was so thin and so darned hard to see-zee.
That he flopped in an armchair which he thought was free-zee
And wheezed, "Oh, alas, my dear, how can this be-zee?
I know you are squished, for I find this chair greasee."

SECOND OPINION

My nurse just told me yesterday,
"You're far too sick to run and play.
You must stay in your room all day!
Have you anything to say?"
"You may be right," I said, "But first
I think I'll ask another nurse."

EWE — TEA — CUSS

When Saint Paul preached in Eff-ee-suss,
A sleepy man named Ewe-tea-cuss
Thought he preached redick-cue-less-lee long.
As Ewe-tea-cuss was sitting in the window of the church,
He rubbed his eyes and yawned and swayed
And nodded, dozed, and reeled and lurched.

And feeling faint, he fell asleep
And fell…and fell for forty feet.
He flopped and flipped and floundered,
Falling, falling, falling downward
Till he hit the fatal flagstones
Of the old Ephesian street.

And Paul felt most embarrassed
(And his face was really red)
That his sermon had gone on so long
That Ewe-tea-cuss was dead.

He laid his hands on Ewe-tea-cuss
And cried, "Be resurrected, friend!
Come back alive. I promise you
I'll never preach so long again."

And Ewe-tea-cuss began to breathe
And opened up his eyes and said,
"Paul…How very nice you're here,
Your sermon really knocked me dead."

Paul really beamed from ear to ear
When Ewe-tea-cuss took a deep breath
Because no preacher wants it known
He preached a healthy man to death.

FANG McNOODLE

My dentist always sings to me
While drilling out my cavities.
He says, "How are you, little one?"
And puts the buzzer in my gum.
And as his drill vibrates my frame
And jars my novocaine-numb brain,
He always sings — it's really strange —
"Drill…spit-a-bit…home on the range…"

I somehow wish he wouldn't sing —
My dentist, Doctor Fang McNoodle —
Still, he's better than my last,
Who drilled and whistled "Yankee Doodle."

QUEEN KONG

On the hundred thirteenth floora
Sweet Queen Kong of Bora Bora
Had a very lovely wedding
Where she proudly purred, "I do."
But when she pledged, "In life or death,"
She blew her guests with monkey breath
In gale-force halitosis and
… Away her guests all flew.

IRIS

"Iris," said God, "It's time to wake up!"
And he rapped on her little brown bulb…

"Oh, hi there! How are you, God?
Is it springtime? It must be!
The ground is so wonderf'ly warm!
I'd hoped to get up by the middle of March —
I'm quite sorry, God, if I've overslept."

Then God called aloud to the newly-born flower,
"Never mind, Iris, get up and get going,
I won't have you napping till May."

"I'm quite wide awake, and I'm tingly with spring,"
Said Iris to God, and she shouted, "Ker-boing!
Yoo-hoo, I'm here, God! Heigh-ho! And sproing! Sproing!
I'm Iris! I'm up! I've shattered the ground,
I'm bursting with life, I've come back to town.
I'm one of the good blooms the ground can't hold down.
Can you see me here, God? I've popped through the sod.
I'm waving! Wave back! If you're there, smile and nod!"

"Yes, Iris, I see you! My, my, you seem free!
You're giddy and pleased with yourself, I can see!
Bloom and grow, Iris—be all you can be!
But tell me, dear Nub, how you feel about me?"

"Really now, God, can you be that important?
I bless every rain and the afternoon sun
And the fuzzy gold bees that tickle my leaves."

"But I made the rain and the sun and the bees,
And you as well, Iris—so, what about me?"

"Dear God—about you I simply don't know,
And I never discuss my religion, you know…
I only know, God, when I get my head
I'm going to shine purple and dance in the sun
And sing a grand hymn to my bright royal glory!
I'll show all those squatty and goggle-eyed marigolds
How stupid and stunted and stinky they are!"

"Never be arrogant, Iris, dear Nub
Because you're so slender and tall,
Remember, all blooms have their weaknesses, dear."
But when God had gone, Iris tried very hard
To think of a weakness that she herself had.
"It's just no use," Iris said to herself.
"My weaknesses all must be far underground.
Oh, I may have a wart on some minor root,
But weaknesses…never!
While God's usually as right as he's wonderfully strong,
This may be the very first time God's been wrong."

She soon was excited to find her green body
Was growing a large purple head
That softly, then firmly unfolded.
She then gazed in glory upon her reflection
In a silver and sky-imaged pool.
She turned her orchid-like head to the sky,
"God, it's Iris again. Just look at me now.
The word to describe me can only be *wow!*"

"Iris," said God, "I must ask you again,
How do you feel about me?"

Iris said nothing — she'd nothing to say.
God pitied Iris and then turned away
And didn't come back till September
And Iris was most glad to see him.

"Hello, God, heigh, ho! I'm Iris the tall!
I'm here where I've always been, here by the wall,
Gazing at autumn: I just love the fall!
I feel like an empress so royal and tall,
As I gaze at the reds of the marigold beds
With scarlets untold and carmines and golds."

"Poor, foolish Iris! You're one braggy bloom!
Be silent, and now, for we do have to talk.
The winter is coming, the season of death."

"You're so very gloomy — what's into you, God?
Think positive! God, whatever you do,
I'm number one...or...perhaps number two.
I can deal with winter, I'm Iris!"

"Iris, please trust me — It's just as I said.
You'll die-you will see-in this garden bed!"

God was then silent for thirty-three days
Till Iris awoke in October:
"Oh God…oh, ouch, oh…ouch…and owee!
God, help! What's this white stuff?
It's freezing! It's burning! It's all over me!"

"Iris, it's frost!
I thought you liked autumn."

"Well, I don't like this frost. Get it off me, God!
I can't stand the pain!"

"Iris, I told you
The winter is coming—the season of death!
You will live again, Iris, but not till the breath
Of the winter wind ends.
The blizzard will cut you and slice your green arms
And freeze your slim stem till it snaps at the ground.
In the pain of your passing you'll beg just to die
And curse your own Maker and look at the sky
And hurl your insults at heaven."

"Never!" cried Iris.

But November blew cold and Iris was buried.

"Help God! Please help! I'm choking in snow.
Oh, why was I born to suffer like this?
If you really are God, you must have some power.
Call off this ice instantly! Now! Do you hear?
Look, you dead marigolds, Iris the fair
Is dying in ice and her God doesn't care."

Bit by bit, Iris froze until finally
She was stiffly encrusted in ice.
She whimpered and whispered,
"My pain is too great; I just cannot bear it.
I'm dying, yes dying…oh, let me die, please…"
She trembled and shuddered and yielded to ice
And snow through the nights drifted silent and cold.
God cried and his tears freezing high in the sky
Fell on His Iris as white.

But the robins of springtime hurried the winter
And the snow once again seeped wet by the wall
And the soft April sun soon smiled the world warm,
Till God rapped again on Iris's root.

"Iris," said God, "It's time to wake up!"

"Oh, hi there...Good morning.
Is it springtime already?
Oh God—I am wiser and now I can see.
It is you I must love and not focus on me.
Oh God, I'm alive...alive and so free!
The ground is so warm—did you warm it for me?"

God only smiled as Iris broke through
And reached her leaves forth through chocolate sod
And waved her green arms and breathed the word, *God*.
This one simple word for her was a prayer,
And sometimes she sang it to brighten the air.
And the marigolds loved her! Each one of them said
That Iris knew how to bend her proud head.
She truly loved God,
For he'd come as he said
And kissed her alive from the dead.

082

COMPUTER

I fed in Yakky software to
Get all the wacky, yakky facts
Of vision problems often found
In many cross-eyed wacky yaks.

In nineteen thousand printed sheets—
Five trillion billion words or so—
I had more facts on cross-eyed yaks
Than I would ever care to know.

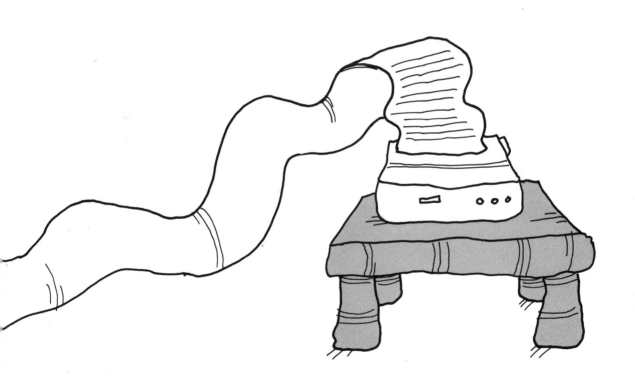

184

MARRIAGE COUNSELOR

"I love you my sweet little dipsy dear duck,"
Said the broad-chested, macho-made platypus hunk.
"Your sweet little quack is a kissy-billed smack:
A joy that I think I have dreamed of or thunk!
   Please marry me,
   marry me,
   marry me, please!
Think it over my sweet; I must know today.
Are you thinking, dear dipsy? Please! What do you say?"

"Let me think. Do not rush. I must have more time.
You rascal, you muscle-bound strong demigod…
All right — I'm through thinking, I'll marry you now.
You Hercules, Atlas, you big handsome dog!
  I'll marry you,
  marry you,
  marry you true.
Our marriage will be quite the envy of all,
Or at least be the goal of just one or two."

When a duck and a platypus wed, things get tough.
She quackily nagged and she never shut up.
Her incessant chatter destroyed his napping.
He spent the night snoring and slapped his broad tail
And kept her awake with snorting and snapping.
  "Our marriage,
  Our marriage,
  Our marriage is sour,
Let's buy some psychiatry this very hour,
Or at least let's admit that our marriage is sour."

The counselor tied her loose beak in a rag,
Which cut out her flap-slappy incessant quack!
He tied-up the platypus's slap-flappy tail,
Which gave him some pain in the small of his back.
And after their counsel they both lived in peace —
    Clap-happy,
    Nap-happy,
    Slap-happy, indeed.
In spite of her bondage and his tied-up tail,
Their marriage seemed no longer destined to fail.

The platypus grew less handsome in time,
But said to his duck, feeling overly lucky,
"Marriages sure have some tough ups and downs;
Still, over a lifetime, they're ducky!
    They're ducky,
    Plum ducky—
    Darn ducky, I'd say;
Get the rag off your beak and kiss me, my sweet,
You're mine from your bill to your yellow webbed feet."

NAMES

My mother, it is clear to see, was very fond of Bible names.
My brother's Mordecaiah Nicodemus Zachariah James.
My mother named my little sis — and this will surely
    hurt your head —
Ruth Zilpah Bilpah Zippora Mary Sarah Jocabed.
I'm the first of triplets three, and here's the handle she
    gave me:
Jeremiah Isaachar Reuben bar Hilkiah.
The other two are: Jonadab Amos Ben Milchaiah
And Hananeel Megiddo Joel Azariah.

My mother loved those Bible names, it's really very true,
But I have always wondered why. Her name is Cindy Sue.

INDEX

192